HEAVEN

JOSEPH BAYLY

LifeJourney Books David C. Cook Publishing Co. Elgin, Illinois

LifeJourney Books is an imprint of
David C. Cook Publishing Co.
Elgin, Illinois and Weston, Ontario
Text, Copyright © 1977 by David C. Cook Publishing Co.
Art, Copyright © 1987 by Timothy R. Botts
First printing, 1987
ISBN 1-55513-296-0
52969/A5225

WHEN their son died unexpectedly, Joseph and Mary Lou Bayly received comfort and help from a poem sent to them by the young woman their son loved and planned to marry. The poem was "New Year, 1945," written by Dietrich Bonhoeffer. Bonhoeffer, imprisoned by the Nazis, had written the poem for his fiance—just three months before he was executed.

Then, 30 years after Bonhoeffer's death and 12 years after their son's—Joe and Mary Lou received a letter from a young Massachusetts pastor. He told of frequently visiting a woman seriously ill in a Boston hospital, and one day giving her an earlier edition of this book, *Heaven*. The next day the woman told the pastor that she had stayed awake late the previous night to read it, and told of the comfort and help she had received from it. Shortly afterward she died.

The woman, the pastor added, had emigrated from Germany after World War II. She was Dietrich Bonhoeffer's fiance, for whom the poem which had comforted the Baylys had been written.

It's six-thirty on a Tuesday morning.
Here I am waiting.
Waiting to be wheeled into an operating room at
Mayo Clinic's Methodist Hospital.
For some reason I am at the beginning of the long line of carts,
soon to number thirty, each holding another human being
who also waits.

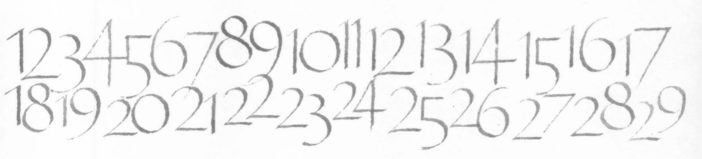

Next to me is a man in his eighties,
beyond him a man younger than I.
The older man is asleep, the younger is himself a medical
doctor. I learn this when another stops to talk briefly with him.
"Does being a doctor help at a time like this?" I ask.
"Not really," he answers, with a wry smile. "It's a mixed bag."

A nurse stops at the head of my cart,
reads the piece of adhesive tape on my forehead,
then asks, "What's your name?"
"Bayly," I answer. "Joseph Bayly."
She moves to the sleeping older man next to me,
reads his name, but doesn't disturb him.
Then on to the doctor, and so down the line.
As people are wheeled past me to take their places
farther down, I nod or smile at the ones who are
still awake. Otherwise I wait.

For what?

I wait for the merciful anesthesia,
then the surgeon, and then...
to come back to consciousness in the room
where dear Mary Lou, my wife of thirty-two winters
and summers - also waits.
Or to come back to consciousness
in the presence of my Lord Christ.

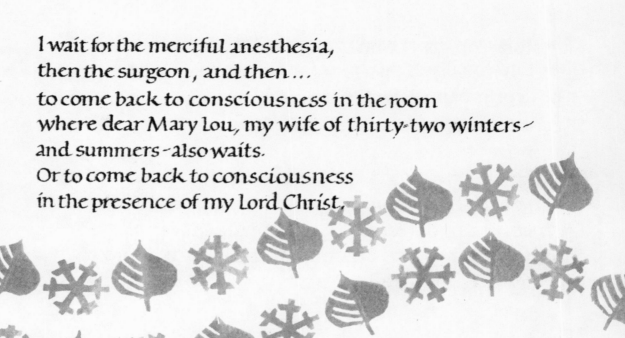

The surgery will not be very serious, there is little risk, but I am equally at peace, as far as I can plumb the depths of my heart, with either prospect.

I wonder how many others in the long white line have this hope. How would I feel, approaching the radical surgical procedures some of them face, without it? Would I have their courage?

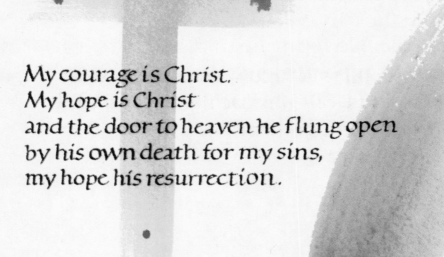

My courage is Christ.
My hope is Christ
and the door to heaven he flung open
by his own death for my sins,
my hope his resurrection.

What will heaven be like, whether I go there
as a result of this operation (a remote possibility),
or go there later (a certainty)?
Heaven will be my eternal home with Christ.
I'll just move into the part of his Father's house
he prepared for me. No fixing up that home, no parts
unfinished, no disappointments on moving day.
No, he's prepared it, he's made it completely ready,
completely perfect, completely mine.

What's a home like, one that he prepares?
A place of peace and beauty, of joy and glory,
of celestial music, of fresh, unchanging, purest love.
I'll say: Hello, Lord. I'm tired.
And he'll say:

REST

because I have work for you to do.

Rest?

Yes, remember that I myself rested
on the seventh day of creation.
So rest is not incompatible with
heaven's perfection.

And work?

Of course.
Did you think heaven would be
an eternal Sunday afternoon nap?

My people serve me in heaven. I have work for you to do.

Keeping all the gold polished?

Ruling Angels.

MANAGING THE UNIVERSE FOR ME

Some day, being responsible for whole cities.

Whole cities? Like New York and Toronto?

LIKE·THEM·IF·EVERYONE·WERE·LIVING
·FOR·MY·GLORY·EVERY·PERSON·SAFE
HARLEM·WITH·TREES·GROWING·IN·IT
and a river of pure water running through it,
AND·PEOPLE·LAUGHING

I remember how he wept over Jerusalem.
And Las Vegas without people desperately trying
to be happy?

HAPPY·WITHOUT·TRYING

Those golden streets . . .

What about them?

Why gold? Not for show, maybe for beauty?

EVERYTHING IN HEAVEN IS TURNED
UPSIDE DOWN FROM EARTH. VALUES
ARE REVERSED. WHAT'S MOST IMPORTANT
ON EARTH? WHAT HAVE MEN LIVED AND
DIED FOR, FOR MILLENNIA?

Gold.

You'll walk on it in heaven. Like concrete or asphalt.

Can I see my sons who died a few years ago?
And my parents, Mary Lou's parents? My brother?

Of course you'll see them.
All of them trusted me on earth.

Except John, the infant. He couldn't understand.
So he couldn't believe.

But he's in heaven because of my atoning work.

Will I recognize them?

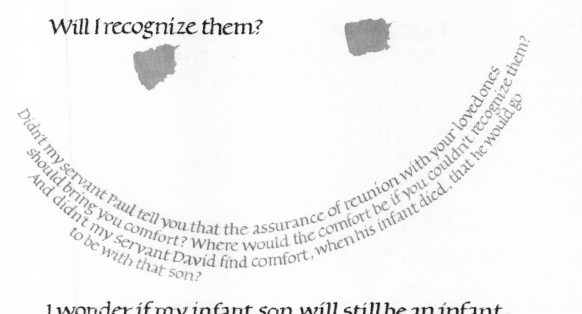

Didn't my servant Paul tell you that the assurance of reunion with your loved ones should bring you comfort? Where would the comfort be if you couldn't recognize them? And didn't my servant David find comfort, when his infant died, that he would go to be with that son?

I wonder if my infant son will still be an infant,
my son who was eighteen when he died still eighteen?

You'll soon see.

You know, just a few weeks ago, I saw a man I hadn't seen for thirty-five years. And I immediately recognized him, even though he was more than a third of a century older than when I saw him last. The surprising thing was that within ten minutes the image of thirty-five years ago had faded, and I knew him as he is now.

You'll know the ones you love.

How about people like Moses, or Abraham or Stephen?

You'll know them, too.
Didn't my disciples, Peter, James and John,
know Moses and Elijah
on the Mount of Transfiguration?

Wow! I can hardly wait.
But will I recognize them when their bodies...

Are still on earth? Still in the grave?
Yes, you will. Again remember how my disciples
recognized Moses. You'll be as much my son
Joe Bayly as you were on earth. But without your
earthly body. That awaits my return to earth,
and your return with me, when that dead and
disintegrated body will come alive, when you'll
reinhabit it and find the glory of

your new body.

I sort of like that body,
It served me well for all these years.
That's not surprising.
And your angel will guard it in its resting place,
just as angels guarded my body in the period
between my death and resurrection.

I LOVE the body that is my
Spirit's temple during
your life on earth,
THE WHOLE YOU
as well as your spirit that will be in heaven
until your own body's resurrection.

Heaven seems more of a city than anything else.

Yes, it is a city—
not people living in isolation,
like on a vast Texas ranch,
but living together.
Not independent, everyone living his own life,
but living together in perfect love,
Perfect harmony, perfect cooperation.
Some of my children may have lived lonely
lives on earth, but never here in heaven.
Isolation, the ultimate aloneness,
is not for my people, but for those
who would not respond to my spirit,
who would not trust me for life eternal.

Will I really be able to sit down with the Old Testament patriarchs – and the matriarchs – and talk with them?

Yes, you will. Don't you remember that I said people like you, who weren't physical descendants of Abraham and Isaac and Jacob, but who trusted me, would have fellowship with them in the kingdom of heaven,

while their own descendants who refused to receive me would be denied entrance into heaven?

I have a question. Maybe it's sort of presumptuous, Sir,
but you can tell me if it is. Will I bring anything with me,
is there anything in heaven that belongs to me?
Except my children, that is. Or will I come as I was born
the first time, naked, taking nothing with me?

Of course you'll bring something with you, or rather,
part of it will be waiting for you. While the rest is
still to come. Birth into heaven isn't the same as
birth into the world. Here you had preexistence
on earth, there you didn't except during your
growing period in the womb.

AND BY THE WAY, YOU DON'T NEED TO BE
AFRAID TO SAY ANYTHING IN HEAVEN,
THAT IT MAY SEEM PRESUMPTUOUS. YOU'LL
BE KNOWN AS YOU ALSO KNOW OTHERS.
NO NEED TO CONCEAL YOURSELF
ANY LONGER. NO MASKS.
IF YOU WANT TO KNOW ANYTHING,
YOU'LL JUST ASK.
BUT TO ANSWER YOUR QUESTION, YES,
YOU WILL HAVE TREASURES IN HEAVEN.
YOU HAVE TONY AS A TREASURE.

Tony? I don't remember any Tony who would be a treasure.

Tony, the older man you witnessed to on your
first job, while you were still a teenager
in New York City. Tony's in heaven.
He's a treasure.

The very best.

Not necessarily the best treasure. There's also the
treasure of another man who tenderly cared for
his wife in old age, during the ten years she was
totally paralyzed.
There's her treasure of an uncomplaining,
grateful spirit.

THERE'S THE TREASURE OF PURITY – A TEENAGER
WHO KEPT HIMSELF FROM THE WORLD'S STAIN,
WHO DID NOT OBEY THE LUSTS OF HIS FLESH.

THERE'S THE TREASURE OF AN
IMPORTANT MAN who remained meek
in all his relationships.

AND THE TREASURE OF PARENTS WHO WERE
FAITHFUL IN RAISING THEIR CHILDREN,
sacrificing their own independence and gratification
for them.

THERE ARE ALMOST LIMITLESS TREASURES
LIMITLESS TREASURES
LIMITLESS TREASURES
LIMITLESS TREASURES
· FOR PEOPLE IN HEAVEN ·

How about money?

NOBODY BRINGS HIS MONEY WITH HIM.

BUT MANY HAVE SENT IT ON AHEAD.

THERE ARE SOME SOUTH AMERICAN INDIANS HERE

WHO LOOK FORWARD TO MEETING YOU.

YOU HELPED SUPPORT THE MISSIONARY WHO TOOK THE GOSPEL

TO THEM, WHO INTRODUCED THEM TO ME.

Are all those things the "gold, silver and precious stones"
the Bible talks about?

Yes, but *don't* look for precisely what my servants
said in the Bible about heaven.

What do you mean?

I was limited in what I could reveal to them,
limited to what their eyes had seen and their
language could express. Can you imagine the
difficulty of describing a *pineapple* to an
ESKIMO ON THE ARCTIC TUNDRA?
SWEET AND JUICY BLUBBER is about as close as
you could come.

Or how could you describe ICE to a DESERT TRIBE?
How could I tell earth people about *heaven?*

What about the Bible writers who had visions?

They had the same problem of communicating what
they saw to others who had not shared their vision.
How would the Eskimo describe a pineapple to others
in his village, even if he were transported to Hawaii
and then returned? "Sweet and juicy blubber" is still
about as close as he could come. I remember how
frustrated my beloved disciple John was as he tried
to describe his vision of the future and of heaven.

So it's far beyond what the Bible says.

Far, far beyond.

How could a twin born into earth world describe what he saw, just in the delivery room even, to his twin not yet born? And beyond the delivery room would be the

ROCKY MOUNTAINS,

THE SKY ON A STARRY NIGHT,

ANIMALS ON AN
AFRICAN GAME FARM

Maybe that's why Isaiah's vision and Daniel's descriptions
of the great beasts always seemed so strange to me,
and a lot of things in Revelation. I could never get a clear
sight on what angels looked like.

You'll soon see them.
And they won't seem strange any longer,
just beautiful and full of power,
like all that I create.

I'll have a lot to see.

It will take you ages to see it.

And to learn?

YOU'LL BE LEARNING AND GROWING FOREVER.

THE STRUCTURE OF THE ATOM IS CHILD'S
PLAY COMPARED TO WHAT YOU'LL LEARN HERE.
AND DID YOU THINK YOU UNDERSTOOD
THE MYSTERY OF MY INCARNATION?
THE PROBLEM OF PAIN?
YOU HAVEN'T BEGUN.

I can hardly wait to study all of human history on earth
from your standpoint, Sir, with all the facts available.

This work you mentioned earlier.
Will it just be managing your universe?

OF COURSE NOT.

You can also plant a garden ,,
without sweat or drought or weeds,
Like Eden. You'll find grass on the other side of the fence
that really is greener.

Or you can create a poem or an oratorio.
You can carve wood
or paint a landscape.

To praise you.

Everything in heaven is to my praise.

MY PEOPLE INTEND IT, SO I ACCEPT IT.
BUT THAT DOESN'T MEAN THAT THEY
ONLY SING MY PRAISE—THEIR WORK
IS PRAISE TO ME.

Will I be able to sing? I've wanted to, since I was a child.

Handel's choir always has room for one more. But for that
matter, you may want to have your own choir, or learn to conduct
it—or an orchestra.

There'll hardly be enough hours in the day to do what I'll want to do.

THERE'S NO NIGHT IN HEAVEN

YOU WON'T NEED TO SLEEP. YOU NEEDED SLEEP ON EARTH FOR RESTORATION OF YOUR STRENGTH OF YOUR DISSOLVING POWERS. BUT IN HEAVEN THERE WILL BE NO WASTING AWAY, NO DISSIPATION OF ENERGY.

Is there any group, any people,
whose entrance into heaven brings you special joy?

The persecuted of earth,
men and women who are imprisoned,
tortured, killed for my sake.
When my servant Stephen was stoned,
I stood to welcome him into glory.
So I welcome all who are faithful
unto death.

What a great thing— to be freed from all persecution
at last. To be totally victorious.

But not just my persecuted ones.
Everyone in heaven will be freed from
all kinds of evil.
There are no guns in heaven,
no bombs, no drunkenness
or violence or war.
AND THE DOORS DON'T HAVE
LOCKS ON THEM
All these things that make earth life fearful for so many people
are forever gone

How about people who weren't able to do things on earth—
the severely handicapped, mongoloid and retarded people?

THEY ARE
my
greatest
joy
IN HEAVEN
NEXT TO THOSE WHO WERE MARTYRED
FOR MY SAKE · TO SEE THEM WHOLE.
ABLE TO DO EVERYTHING THEY COULDN'T DO
ON EARTH...TO THOSE WHO HAD NOT
IT HAS BEEN GIVEN

"And from those who had, it shall be taken" –
does that mean that the geniuses on earth,
the ones who had great power and great gifts,
but never turned to you in simple faith –
does that mean their gifts are now taken away?

Yes, hell is a place of

TOTAL LOSS

The world-famous violinist
WHO TURNED FROM ME IS
TONE DEAF,

THE PHYSICIST can't manage
an abacus,

THE WORLD LEADER
has no one to control.
For them that is unending sorrow.
And it is unending sorrow to me.
How often I would have
gathered them into
my family on earth,
but they would not consent to be gathered

They must have an awful lot of regret, of "if only" feelings,
How about in heaven - will I think "if only"?

If you do, I shall wipe away your tears,
Sorrow is forever gone.
You will not face the past,
but the future.

Are there many people in heaven?

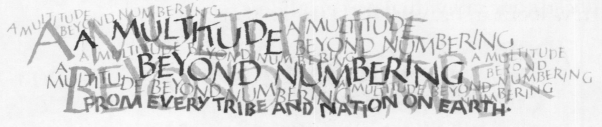

A MULTITUDE BEYOND NUMBERING FROM EVERY TRIBE AND NATION ON EARTH.

Can they understand each other?

THEY SPEAK ONE LANGUAGE, AS IT WAS BEFORE BABEL.

It seems to me that a lot of things are the way
you originally intended earth to be.

Yes, but different, better,
even as I excel the first Adam.

If there's such a great crowd in heaven,
doesn't one individual person get lost, or absorbed?

THERE'S A GREAT CROWD ON EARTH
TOO, AND YET YOU'RE DIFFERENT FROM
EVERY OTHER PERSON WHO EVER LIVED.
EVEN YOUR FINGERPRINTS ARE
DIFFERENT.
YOU'LL BE THE SAME *unique you*
IN HEAVEN

AND YOU'LL BE UNIQUELY MINE—
I CALL EVERYONE BY NAME.
MOSES IS MOSES, PRISCILLA IS PRISCILLA,
AND YOU'LL BE JOSEPH BAYLY THROUGHOUT
ETERNITY.

I'm ashamed to admit it, but I'm a little scared.
I really like this world: the Rocky Mountains,
the beach at Cape May, the fields behind our house,
the barn through mist on a gray wintry morning.
How can I adjust to heaven when it's so different?

That World
you like,
it is
but a womb

A womb?

Yes, you may not
perceive it in that way
but you are bound within
earthworld as surely as a baby yet
unborn is bound
within the womb

Maybe
the baby
would be
scared to be
born, to leave the womb.

Then death is...

DELIVERANCE to LIFE BEYOND YOUR IMAGINING

The death incident is merely a passage from earth life, from the womb that has contained you until now, into the marvelous newness of heaven life. You'll go through a dark tunnel, you may experience pain–just as you did when you were born a baby–but beyond the tunnel is heaven. I promise you, you'll enjoy heaven.

And I'll enjoy you.

Somehow in our conversation I've gotten so excited about what a wonderful place heaven is that I've almost forgotten you, forgotten that eternal life is to know you, Lord Jesus, that your presence makes heaven heaven.

That's all right—
a child sees all of life with a child's eyes.

BUT IN HEAVEN, YOU WILL BE FULL-GROWN,
YOU WILL BE PERFECTLY MATURE.

Then you will learn to worship and praise and be thankful.

NOW YOU STAND ON A MOUNTAIN, LIKE MY SERVANT MOSES,
FROM WHICH YOU CAN SEE
the wilderness of your earth life
AND
the approaching happiness
of the promised land
BOTH AT THE SAME TIME.
DO YOU FIND YOUR PERSPECTIVE CHANGING?

I do, I surely do. Some things I enjoyed seem to be fading
away as I see heaven in the distance. Others are vastly
more important. My values seem to be changing. I may
not long for death, but I surely long for heaven.